FOR AS LONG AS I CAN REMEMBER,

I WANTED TO BE A PROFESSIONAL

HOCKEY PLAYER.

mario lemieux

the final period

PHOTOGRAPHY BY MARC SEROTA

EDITED BY TOM MCMILLAN

PRODUCED BY

rareAIR
A MARK VANCIL COMPANY

ADDITIONAL PHOTOS

Lemieux Archive Photos
Courtesy of the Lemieux Family
pgs. 1, 10, 15-20, 23 (wedding), 39.

Colin Braley-Reuters
pgs. 47 (bottom), 58, 59.

Peter Diana
Pittsburgh Post-Gazette
pgs. 12, 13, 21, 36, 37, 39, 45, 92,
96-99.

Karen Meyers
pg. 6.

Bruce Bennett Studios
pgs. 40 (top), 42, 54-55, 104-107.

Pittsburgh Penguins
pgs. 43, 47, 64, 75, 79 (top), 85.

PITTSBURGH PENGUINS:

Tom McMillan, Steve Bovino,
Tommy Plasko, Howard Baldwin,
Denny Cavanaugh and the
entire Pens organization.

SPECIAL THANKS

The Lemieux Family—Mr. Jean-Guy & Mrs. Pierrette Lemieux,
Alain, Richard, Nathalie, Lauren, Stephanie, Austin and our baby to be...
Steve Reich, Tom Reich, Donald "Dee" Rizzo, Maryann, Chuck
Greenberg and the entire Reich, Brisson & Reich Staff.
Joe Deloria at CANON EOS Cameras, Jim Olsen at FUJI Film—
the exclusive supplier of film for this project, Craig Davis & Barbara
Curley at Westin William Penn for accommodations, Jeff Flynn &
Gene Smith at UPI Marketing, Joseph R. Faccenda & John Tedesco
at Giant Eagle, Ray & John Curley at LaRussa Foods, Mitch Rogatz
& Michael Emmerich at Triumph Books, John Hayt, Dan Marino &
Mr. Daniel C. Marino Sr., Ann Fulton, Cindi & Larry Richert, The Molson
Family, Koho, KDKA and the City of Montreal, Canada.

THE MARIO LEMIEUX FOUNDATION

TOM BARRASSO, ASHLEY BARRASSO AND MARIO LEMIEUX.

The Mario Lemieux Foundation was formed in July 1993 to
assist cancer research programs. The foundation's support is available to organizations and research hospitals throughout the United
States and Canada.

"As I went through the treatments for Hodgkin's disease in the
winter of 1993, I began to realize how fragile life can be," Mario
said. "I felt that I had to give something back to the community, and
this is when I decided to form the Lemieux Foundation."

One of the foundation's major fund-raising projects is an annual
summer golf tournament that began in 1995.

"Mario's decision to proceed with the foundation is a reflection
of his ongoing concern for others," said Penguins owner Howard
Baldwin, a member of the foundation's board.

Contributions may be made to the Mario Lemieux Foundation,
2300 Gulf Tower, 707 Grant Street, Pittsburgh, PA 15219.

A Tribute

Virtually all of the accolades—in every language—already have been written and spoken about Mario Lemieux. The Michelangelo of hockey has etched his artistic brilliance on the surface of every major ice palace in North America.

Along with millions of other passionate hockey fans, I always will be able to retrieve in my mind's eye any one of the endless examples of his hockey genius. More importantly, I will remember Mario Lemieux for the eloquence of his responses to a never-ending succession of physical ailments that interrupted this career throughout the 1990s.

The various diseases and structural injuries that ravaged him were consistently met by a series of recoveries and comebacks unprecedented in professional sports. The quality of performance throughout this entire traumatic period could only have been exceeded by the measure of his fortitude and uncompromising dignity.

We thank you, Mario, for the rinkside seat to the Greatest Show on Ice, which produced such towering accomplishments in the face of excruciating obstructions. None of us could aspire to your art, but for myself, I am a better person for having witnessed your courageous and unforgettable journey.

With the most profound respect and great admiration, your friend…

Tom Reich

I WOULD LIKE TO DEDICATE this pictorial autobiography to the people closest to me, the people who have made great sacrifices to enable me to enjoy an outstanding career—my parents, my wife, and, of course, my children.

My parents, JEAN-GUY AND PIERRETTE, were totally supportive of my hockey career from the time I first stepped on the ice back home in Montreal. I couldn't have achieved anything without them.

My wife, NATHALIE, always has been there for me, providing love, advice and support. During my medical problems, she was the best nurse I ever had. We are having a great time raising our three children—LAUREN, STEPHANIE AND AUSTIN—and are looking forward to our fourth, which is on the way as this is being written.

I also would like to thank my agents, TOM REICH, STEVE REICH AND PAT BRISSON, for their friendship and guidance. They are the ones who made this book possible and allowed me to tell my story.

And TO ALL MY TEAMMATES, from the neighborhood rinks back in Montreal to Pittsburgh and the NHL… thanks for everything.

I TREASURE THE MEMORIES.

MARIO LEMIEUX
JUNE 1997

CONTENTS

chapter one

the personal side

For as long as I can remember, I wanted to be a professional hockey player. The game was my passion from the very first time I picked up a stick and a puck.

Like most kids who grew up in the Montreal area, I started skating when I was about three years old; hockey is the most important sport in all of Canada, but in the province of Quebec, and especially in our little suburb of Ville Emard, it was almost a religion.

My parents, Jean-Guy and Pierrette, were big fans of the Montreal Canadiens and my older brothers, Alain and Richard, already had been on skates by the time they took me to the little rink behind St-Jean de Matha church, a few blocks from our house on Rue Joques.

I used a chair for balance like all the other beginners, but my parents tell me that I let go of the chair after about 10 minutes. I was skating on my own. MAYBE IT WAS DESTINY.

Anyway, skating—and hockey—quickly became a part of me. I remember coming back from school, putting my skates on, skating to the rink and playing there until it was 8 or 9 o'clock at night, before coming home to do my homework. It seemed like I did the same thing every day. I skated for four or five hours. It was a natural thing, something I enjoyed doing, and that stayed with me throughout my career.

I was probably five or six years old when I understood the concept of a professional player, when I realized that, if you were good enough, you could do this for a living. From that point on, it's all I wanted to do. That didn't set me apart from the other kids in our neighborhood, or in Montreal, or in the province; hockey was everything to us.

BUT AS I LOOK BACK, I KNOW THE SEEDS OF MY CAREER WERE PLANTED AT A VERY EARLY AGE.

People often have asked me when I realized that I might have a special talent for the game, and I can honestly say that it was when I was eight or nine years old. I guess you don't really have a sense of how you compare to other kids at that age, but I began to score five or six goals a game on a regular basis, and that was unusual. There were a lot of people from different parts of Montreal coming down just to see me. As far as I can remember, we always had big crowds.

One of my biggest thrills as a young player came when I was about 12, and Scotty Bowman, the coach of the Canadiens, came to one of our games. I was told he was in the stands especially to look at me. And it's ironic how things work out; Scotty came to work for the Pittsburgh Penguins in 1990 and coached us to our second straight Stanley Cup championship in 1991-92.

I PLAYED FOR A LOCAL TEAM CALLED
THE HURRICANES
FROM THE TIME I WAS SEVEN UNTIL
I REACHED MIDGET AGE AT 15.

So I spent eight years with the Hurricanes, playing with and against some very talented kids who would go on to make the NHL.

Marc Bergevin was my left winger for a while. J.J. Daigneault, who later became my teammate in Pittsburgh, was one of our best skaters.

I remember playing against big Sergio Momesso throughout my youth hockey career, and then we became teammates one season in

midget AAA, before I got drafted to play major junior.

HOCKEY ALWAYS WAS THE CENTERPIECE OF OUR LIVES.

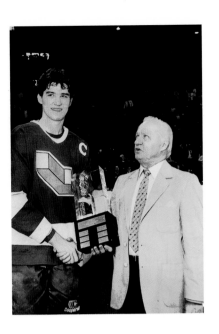

Even when there weren't organized games, we played on the local rinks, we played in the street, we played in the basement. My brothers and I used to scrape the ceiling of the basement with our sticks when we were celebrating goals, pretending to be NHL players.

And then there is the story—reported in several newspapers and magazines—about my mother's penchant for packing snow in the hallway of our house so that Alain, Richard and I could skate. Well, I'm here to tell you that, crazy as it sounds, that story is true. She got a little bit of snow and we'd put on our skates and go skating on the carpet. It wasn't like a rink or anything—it was just the effect of having some snow there. I don't think it did anything to improve our skating, but, hey, it's a good story.

We also used to watch the games on television whenever we could. One Saturday night, when our parents went out to dinner, one of our cousins came over to babysit the three of us, but she had a rule that we couldn't watch hockey. Unfortunately for her, she made the mistake of going to the bathroom. So I locked her in there, and we didn't let her out until the end of the game.

As I said, HOCKEY MEANT EVERYTHING TO THE PEOPLE OF MONTREAL—ESPECIALLY TO THE LEMIEUX BOYS.

THE LEMIEUXS OF VILLE EMARD

I've had a strong sense of family since I was very young, because my parents instilled it in me. In our little Montreal suburb of Ville Emard, we probably had 10 families of relatives within two blocks, and we were always together. Brothers, cousins, uncles. It seemed like you could go to any street in the community and find one of our relatives.

My parents still live in the same house I grew up in—the same duplex they've owned since they were married almost 40 years ago. I've been fortunate to do very well financially in my career, and I've offered many times to buy them a

newer, bigger house in another part of town. I'm still offering. But my mother's got her sister and her entire extended family there, and she's used to the same things all the time, the same routine. I think she's afraid to move because she would miss the house and all the memories. That's the key, I guess. All the memories are there.

Alain is five years older than me. As the oldest of the three boys, he blazed the hockey trail for our family, developing into a star in the Quebec Major Junior Hockey League and getting drafted by the St. Louis Blues. Alain played parts of six seasons in the NHL with St. Louis,

the Quebec Nordiques and the Penguins, scoring 28 goals and 72 points in 119 games (I remember once when he scored a hat trick in an exhibition game for the Penguins, the headline referred to him as the "other" Lemieux). He had good skills and also was a productive scorer at the minor pro level. Since retiring in the early 1990s, he has moved to Pittsburgh and now runs hockey schools throughout the northeast. Richard, who is 16 months older than me, was my youth hockey teammate for four years. He had a big shot but never played professionally. He still lives in Montreal and works for Molson.

My parents are proud of all three boys and we are proud of them; they've had a profound influence on each of our lives.

I know in my case, my mom was available for whatever I needed. She totally supported my hockey career. We used to practice early in the morning, sometimes as early as 5 o'clock, and she used to be the one to get me out of bed, dress me while I was still asleep and take me out to the car. Once I got to the rink, then all I had to do was put my skates on. I was ready to go. Other kids used to have to take the bus at 5 a.m., and most of their parents weren't there because they were work-

ere for us,   skates, but whatever we   my mom makes the parties   their styles.

g plus.   needed was there for us,   and my dad likes to watch the

NATHALIE AND THE KIDS

Nathalie Asselin was 15 years old when I met her through—what else?—a family connection. My cousin is married to her cousin and that's how we got together. Her cousin, who thought we might make a nice couple, brought her down to a game one day and we started going out. I was 16 at the time. I guess you can say the rest is history.

Nathalie came to visit me during my early years in Pittsburgh and then came here to live with me a few years later. We were married in 1993 and now have three children—Lauren, Stephanie and Austin—with a fourth due in the late summer of 1997. We've settled into a new home in the Pittsburgh suburb of Sewickley and also have a place in Florida. And yes, we're teaching both English and French to our kids.

I can't even begin to describe how important Nathalie has been to my life and my career. She's always been very supportive—especially during the tough times, like my back surgery. She's the best nurse I've ever had. I mean, the nurses at the hospital are great, but it's very special when you have a family member caring for you. I was on my back for three months with a serious infection in the fall of 1990 and she was always there, doing all my intravenous procedures, doing whatever I needed to recuperate and get back to playing hockey.

And she loves the game. Like me, she was mesmerized by the Montreal hockey experience and became a big fan of the Montreal Canadiens. And she always enjoyed watching me play. That's one of the reasons she didn't want me to quit hockey for good when I took a year off to rest and recuperate in 1994-95. It was hard for her. And she was a big part of my comeback.

Hockey always was important to us, but our lives changed in a big way—forever—from the time we had Lauren, our first child, in 1993. Having kids changes your

priorities dramatically. No matter what else you do, your kids are the most important thing in your life. Your kids, your health, and then after that, your career. At one point in my life, my career definitely was No. 1. But once we had kids…well, your whole life revolves around what they're doing. And seeing them grow and learn and develop into little people is pure joy.

to help out but I still had to go to the rink, practice, and come back as soon as I could to take care of our two daughters. Fortunately, we were able to keep the whole ordeal out of the media until Austin was born, because that would have created an unnecessary distraction. We chose to deal

We've had our share of adversity, though. Our son, Austin, was born three months premature in March of 1996. That was a very tough experience because Nathalie was in bed for three months. She couldn't get up. Her mother was down here from Montreal

with it privately, as a family. A few teammates and Penguins team officials knew, but that was it.

Once Austin was born and began doing pretty well, we all could give thanks and take a big sigh of relief. And I was able to resume playing at a high

level, with my mind free from worry. I don't think it is a coincidence that I scored five goals against the St. Louis Blues just two days after Austin was born. I guess it was equal parts celebration and elation and relief. Nathalie was incredible, with the way she handled the whole thing.

As I write this, we've got another child—a fourth—on the way. That's probably the last one, although Nathalie will have something to say about it, of course. Nathalie always wanted four or five kids.

FROM MY PERSPECTIVE?
AFTER TESTING LIFE WITH KIDS FOR
THE PAST FOUR YEARS,
I THINK FOUR
WILL BE ENOUGH
(I'M LAUGHING, JUST SO YOU KNOW).

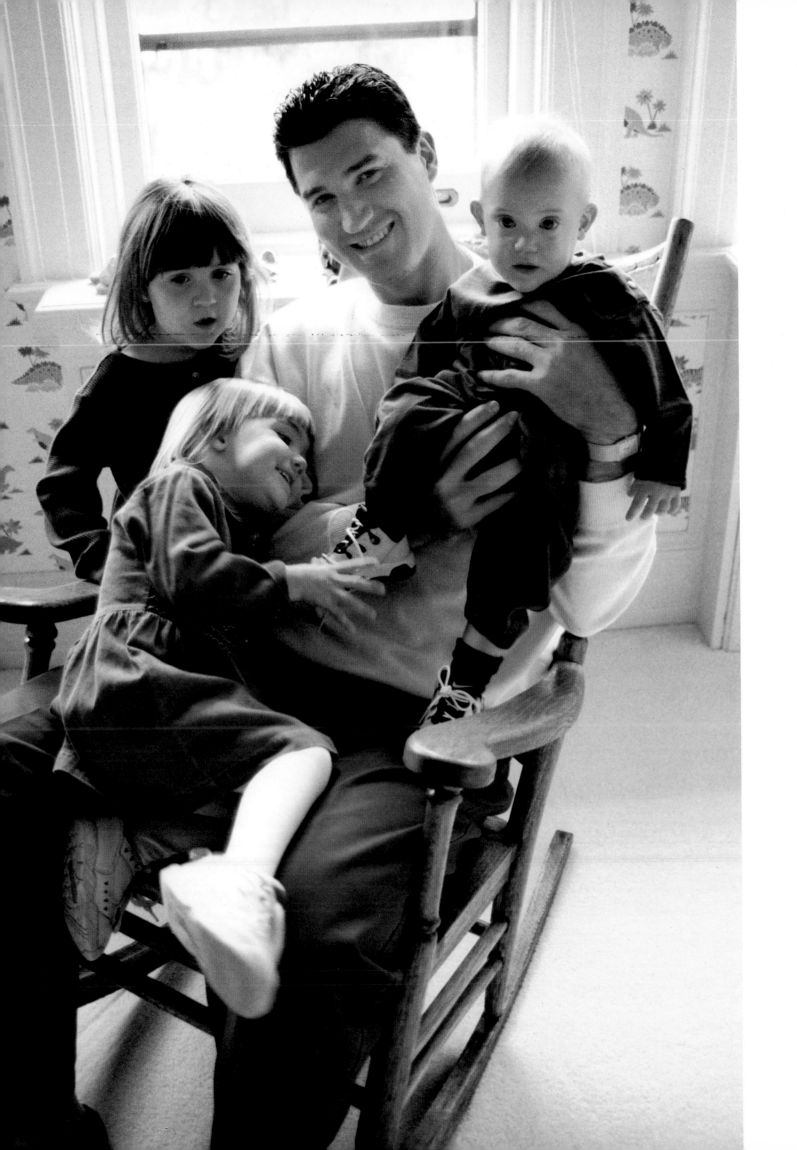

As a family, we love our new home in Sewickley. I think it's important for the family to be in a neighborhood that is well respected and is nice for the kids. Sewickley has one of the best schools in Pittsburgh, and that also was part of our decision. We just wanted to come here and have a little privacy.

My hockey career is over, but I'm going to stay here in Pittsburgh, build my family and raise my kids here. I can't think of a better city than this one. I've traveled all over the world and I feel very comfortable in Pittsburgh. The people are nice, the golf courses are nice. I have a lot of friends here. I've been in Pittsburgh 13 years—all of my adult life—and it would be very difficult for me to move and go somewhere else. I've got everything I need here. And we just like the city. I'm definitely going to spend some time in Florida as well, at our place there, from time to time. But I'm looking forward to spending about nine months out of the year right here in Pittsburgh.

As for the FUTURE?

I always wanted to take a full year off once I was finished playing, and that's what I'm going to do—relax, travel with the family, play a lot of golf, which is my passion. I've been thinking for a long time that I just want to get up in the morning not knowing what to expect. I'll be taking care of the kids, driving them to school, taking part in their activities, all that stuff. I just want to try it for one year and see if I like it.

If not? Then I'm going to look for work.

chapter two
a star on the rise

The most direct route to the NHL for a young prospect is Canadian major junior hockey, and that was the path I chose. In 1981, when I was 16 years old, I was drafted by the Laval Voisins of the Quebec Major Junior Hockey League and began my trek to the big time.

Once I got drafted, I picked 66 as my jersey number. My agents

at the time were Gus Badali and Bob Perno, and they also handled

Wayne Gretzky, who made No. 99 the most unique number in hockey.

For some reason, they threw 66 out there and it made sense to me

at the time. It would be my own number, my own identity.

NO ONE ELSE
IN THE WORLD
WAS WEARING IT.

As far as the pressure because of the comparisons to Gretzky?

I've never minded facing pressure. I've always had a lot of

confidence in my abilities. I agreed that I wanted a number

I had a pretty successful year as a rookie in junior, collecting a nice, neat number of assists—66—to go with 30 goals in 64 games. It was after that season that I made the decision to drop out of school and devote all of my attention to hockey. IN A SENSE, THAT'S WHEN I BECAME A PRO.

The older guys on our team, who already were out of high school, always skated in the morning and then played at night—just like the pros. I knew that I had a pretty good shot at becoming a professional, and I wanted to spend more time at the game, working on my skills. Some people may not have agreed with the decision to quit school, but it was the right one for me.

In my second season of junior hockey, 1982-83, I scored 184 points in 66 games—there's that number again—and was named a second-team all-star in the Quebec league, behind Pat LaFontaine. Pat led the league in scoring that year and was selected third overall in the 1983 NHL entry draft by the New York Islanders. It gave me something to shoot for in the next year, my draft year. I always wanted to be picked No. 1 in the NHL draft, and I knew I had a good shot.

Fortunately for me, I had a season to remember in 1983-84. I scored 133 goals and 282 points in 70 games, leading the league in all categories and establishing Canadian junior records for goals and points that still stand. I set another junior record by scoring at least one point in 61 straight games, was named Canadian Major Junior Player of the Year, led my team to the Quebec league championship and a berth in the Memorial Cup tournament and was ranked as the No. 1 prospect in the draft by NHL Central Scouting.

ONE OF MY **BIGGEST THRILLS**
THAT YEAR WAS HAVING THE OPPORTUNITY
TO BREAK THE JUNIOR
RECORD FOR GOALS IN A SEASON,
HELD BY MY IDOL, GUY LAFLEUR.

Heading into the last game of the season I needed three goals to do it, and I scored six that night—with five assists. Guy was the player I looked up to when I was younger, and I was one of his biggest fans during his career with the Montreal Canadiens. To have a chance to beat one of his records—a record that had stood since the early 1970s—definitely was a highlight for me.

Not that the year went by without controversy. I was picked to represent Canada in the world junior tournament over the Christmas holidays but decided not to attend. I knew I was going to be drafted and turn pro, so this would be my last chance to spend Christmas at home with my parents. In addition, I was trying to set the junior record for most consecutive games with a point— a streak that would have been broken if I'd gone to the world tournament. They tried to stop me but I went to court and we won. So I didn't miss any games, went on to break the record and—very enjoyably— got to spend Christmas at home.

BECOMING A PENGUIN

or the team, but I knew they were interested; Eddie Johnston, the Penguins general manager, attended about eight Laval games that season and made it clear to reporters that he wanted to take me with the first overall pick.

And that was fine with me. When you're drafted No. 1, you're almost certain to go to a weak, struggling team in need of rebuilding. Personally, I looked forward to the challenge. I knew Pittsburgh was the worst team in the league and that it was going to take a few years to get out of the cellar, much less challenge for the Stanley Cup,

but I was anxious for the chance to help build a championship team. I knew I was going to have to be very patient, and I gave myself five years to start doing something, team-wise. All the losing was difficult to accept at first, but it paid off.

As the draft approached, I was aware that several teams, including Montreal and Quebec, were talking to Pittsburgh about

As the 1983-84 junior season was winding down, I paid more and more attention to the NHL standings, to see who would finish last and qualify for the first pick overall. The "battle" was between the Pittsburgh Penguins and the New Jersey Devils, and it looked like Pittsburgh would "win." I didn't know very much about the city

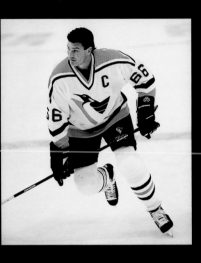

negotiations with the Penguins had reached a stalemate and my agents advised me to break tradition and not go to the Penguins table when my name was called. That meant not putting on my new team's jersey for the publicity photos. Believe me, it caused a stir.

Looking back, I wish I would have done it differently. I was advised to do it that way, but trading for the top pick. Quebec offered all three Stastny brothers. The Minnesota North Stars offered all 12 of their picks. Johnston listened politely before turning them all down, saying that he didn't want to go for a quick fix. He left little doubt that he was going to take me No. 1.

Draft day was in June at the Montreal Forum, and it was a big day for me and my family— although not without another touch of controversy. Contract

sometimes you do things when you're younger that you later regret. That was one of them.

Anyway, we reached a contract agreement with the Penguins about a week later and everything was smoothed over. The Penguins, who had averaged only 6,800 fans a game while going 16-58-6 in the 1983-84 season, began to use me in all their ticket promotions and were hyping the first home game of the regular season as the "Lemieux Debut

Our first game of the season was on the road against the Boston Bruins, meaning

I would break into the NHL in venerable old Boston Garden. I was excited and nervous

and really hoped to make a good showing, but not even I could have dreamed that

I would score a goal in my first game, on my first shift, on my first shot.

FIRST **GAME**

The memory is crystal clear, even 13 years later.

I went to the point and Ray Bourque was there, and

FIRST **SHIFT**

he kind of hurried his shot; it

hit me in the pads and I just

FIRST **SHOT**

kind of snuck by him. The next thing I knew, I had

a breakaway against the Bruins goaltender, Pete

FIRST **GOAL**

Peeters. The whole thing happened so

fast. All of a sudden, I was right beside

Pete Peeters and I didn't know what to do, so I just gave it my

favorite move—and the puck went in! I was so excited to be able

to do that on my first shift in the NHL. It's hard to find the words to

describe it. But that definitely was a great moment in my career.

There also were some highlights during my first home game at the Civic Arena—Oct. 17 against Vancouver. I picked up an assist on my first shift, setting up a goal by Doug Shedden, and

I GOT INTO MY
FIRST NHL FIGHT

with Gary Lupul, who'd been agitating me. The Pittsburgh crowd went crazy, and, after a 4-3 victory, the Lemieux Debut was termed a success. But despite the early excitement, the season was an uphill climb for our team.

We didn't come close to making the playoffs, but we added some good players and improved from 38 to 53 points in the standings. I finished with 43 goals and collected my 100th point on the final day of the regular season against Washington. That was an important achievement because only two players in the history of the game had scored 100 points as rookies, Peter Stastny and Dale Hawerchuk. I was named MVP of the All-Star Game at mid-season and was awarded the Calder Trophy as NHL Rookie of the Year.

In many ways, the adjustments I had to make on the ice that first season were easier than the adjustments off the ice. Although I began

to learn English while playing junior hockey, in anticipation of a pro career, I grew up and lived in a predominantly French environment.

For a while, the new language was a struggle. I took a

Berlitz course just before I came to Pittsburgh—five

hours a day for three weeks—but it was just too much

in a short period of time. When I came here, I watched

a lot of television, especially the soap operas, trying to

pick up the language and learn the meaning of words

and phrases.

EVEN WITH ALL OF THAT,
I DIDN'T FEEL COMFORTABLE
ANSWERING QUESTIONS
FROM REPORTERS AFTER GAMES,

because my English wasn't that good. I was afraid to make mistakes

because I thought people would laugh at me. That, really, was the toughest

part of my rookie year. The hockey was difficult, sure, but dealing with all the

attention and not being able to express myself the way I wanted was even

more difficult. I took a lot of pride in my new language and tried to speak

it as well as I could.

I feel very comfortable with it now, but I still make mistakes from time to time. It's my second language and even after 13 years in the United States, I'm still learning. I still want to improve and work on my accent a bit. But I've come a long way from my first interview as an 18-year-old rookie.

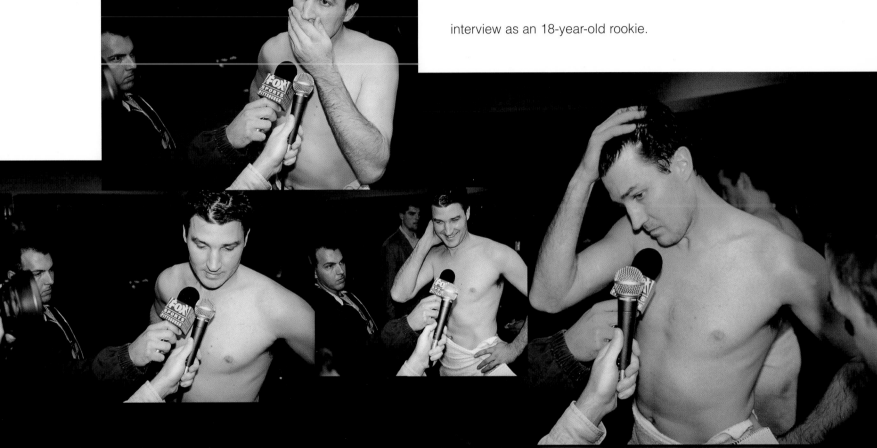

ONE OTHER THING THAT I HAVE TO MENTION: I couldn't have made it through that first year without the help of the Mathews family—Tom, Nancy and their kids. They took me into their home through an arrangement with Eddie Johnston, and that made the whole year a lot easier, having a family that could care for me. Nancy was like a second mom. She cooked my meals and washed my clothes, so I didn't have to worry about that. And she helped teach me a lot about the language. In my second year, I lived on my own, but I was still close to the Mathews family, and Nancy often stopped by to check on me. We remain great friends. I can never repay my debt for what they did for me.

As I progressed through my second and third NHL seasons, I had to keep reminding myself about my vow as a junior—that I would have patience, that it would take at least five years to build a championship contender in Pittsburgh.

In 1985-86, I racked up 141 points to place second behind Wayne Gretzky in the scoring race, and our team came surprisingly close to a .500 record—34-38-8 for 76 points. We finished in fifth place in the Patrick Division, one spot ahead of New Jersey, marking

the first time since 1981-82 that the Penguins hadn't finished last in their division. But the next year I missed 17 games because of injuries, dipped to 107 points and saw us regress a bit in the standings—to 72 points, although still out of the cellar.

THINGS WERE
GOING SLOWLY.

But the summer of 1987 brought with it a real sense of excitement for me and for hockey fans in Canada. The Canada Cup tournament was scheduled for August and September, pitting the top hockey-playing nations against one another in a true battle for world supremacy. And everyone was gearing up for a championship series between Team Canada and the powerful Soviet Union.

It would be difficult to recreate that same feeling in the late

1990s—what with the collapse of the Iron Curtain, the fall of Communism and the influx of Russian and Czech players to the NHL. But back then, there was a sense of anonymity and mystery to the Soviet team, which added to their mystique. They had won several important international competitions in recent years, including an 8-1 blowout over Team Canada in the championship game of the 1981 Canada Cup. The debate raged on as to which country played better hockey.

My only international experience as a professional had come at the end of my rookie season in 1985. I scored two goals to lead Canada to an upset victory over the Soviets at the world championships, and we took home a bronze medal for our efforts. But the annual world championship competition was a watered-down affair because it conflicted with the Stanley Cup playoffs, and most of the top Canadian, American and Swedish stars were busy playing for their NHL teams. That's why there was so much anticipation for the Canada Cup; all the top players would be available to play for their countries, making it the best against the best.

I was genuinely excited about the opportunity to play with great players and legitimately compete for a championship. It would give me a chance to answer critics who wondered how I would play under pressure, and, more importantly, it would give me a chance to learn from the best.

I was especially looking forward to playing with Wayne Gretzky, Mark Messier, Paul Coffey and all the guys from Edmonton who'd been winning Stanley Cups. I really wanted to learn how to win, and they were the best examples. Practicing with those guys for five weeks in a row and seeing the level of intensity that it takes to be a champion certainly improved my game and brought me, personally, to a new level.

the same line until then, but he put us together in the second period of Game 2 and we really clicked. I scored three goals, including the game-winner in double overtime—setting up a winner-take-all Game 3 in Hamilton.

We came from behind to beat Czechoslovakia in the semifinals in Montreal, and I scored one of the goals to help solve their spectacular goaltender, an unknown commodity at the time named Dominik Hasek. That set up a best-of-three championship series with the Soviets, who'd beaten Sweden in the semis.

Purists still call it the best hockey ever played. All three games were decided by one goal and two of them went to overtime. The atmosphere was indescribable.

The Soviets won Game 1 in Montreal, 6-5 in overtime, putting a lot of pressure on us as the series switched to Hamilton. Our coach, Mike Keenan, had resisted suggestions to play Wayne and me on

We fell behind quickly, rallied again, took the lead—only to have Valeri Kamensky, who now plays for the Colorado Avalanche, tie the score at 5-5 with a tremendous individual effort. With less than two minutes to play, however, Keenan sent me out on a line with Wayne and Dale Hawerchuk for a faceoff deep in our defensive zone.

Dale won the draw and I chipped the puck to Wayne, who began carrying it up the left-wing boards. I followed behind him, lurking, and he fed me a great pass inside the blue line to set me up for a chance at hockey immortality. I took my time and ripped a shot

into the upper corner of the net for the game-winner, the tournament-winner—and bedlam broke loose on the ice, in the stands, and all across Canada. Wayne

led the tournament in points and I led in goals, but this was more than just a numbers thing. Scoring those two game-winning goals in the finals certainly gave me a lot of confidence for the rest of my career. It showed that I was able to perform under a lot of pressure against the best

players in the world and be successful, that I could raise my game to another level when the game—and the championship—was on the line.

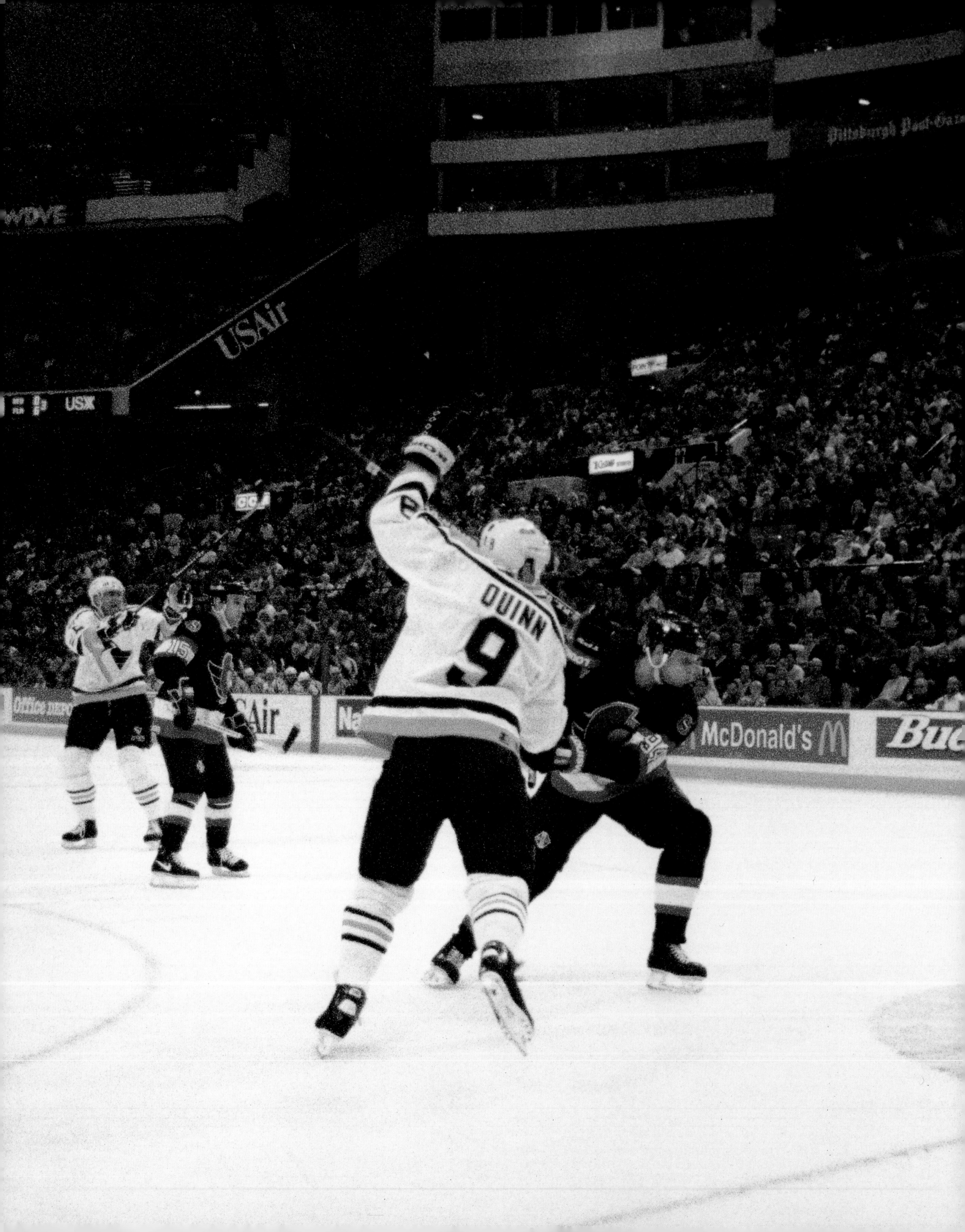

USAir
QUINN
9
McDonald's

I came to Pittsburgh after the tournament in the best shape of my life, bursting with confidence, and I really think it showed. My legs were strong.

the aftermath of the Canada Cup experience.

Another major factor in my improvement as a player and our improvement as a team

I was able to beat guys one-on-one with speed and strength.

I don't think it was any coincidence that I won my first NHL scoring title and my first league MVP award that season, in

came when we acquired Coffey from Edmonton in a November trade. It cost us two good, young prospects—Craig Simpson and Chris Joseph—but "Coff" was the kind of dynamic offensive defenseman we'd always needed. Once we got him it really changed the look of our team, and it really helped me to have somebody

We just clicked. We had good chemistry together.

I led the league with 70 goals and 168 points and we finished over .500 at 36-35-9 for 81

chapter three

overcoming odds

The 1988-89 season turned out to be a big one—both for me, personally, and for our team. I set career highs with 85 goals and 199 points while playing on a line with Rob Brown and Bob Errey, and the Penguins made the playoffs for the first time since 1981-82.

We swept the New York Rangers in the first round of the playoffs, then took the Philadelphia Flyers to seven games in the division finals. I was lucky enough to have a monster game against the Flyers in Game 5 of that series, scoring five goals and eight points to tie two league playoff records. We knew we didn't have the team to win the Cup that year, but it was a good experience for the organization just to get back in the playoffs and see what it took. We definitely built on that.

That season, however, was the last time in my career that I was fully healthy. I played 76 of the 80 games and all 11 playoff games and felt great doing it. But with the next year came some incredible back pain, due to a disk problem, eventually leading to surgery.

My BACK BECAME AN ISSUE FOR THE REST OF MY CAREER.

6

MOST POINTS IN ONE ALL-STAR GAME

ALL-STAR GAME RECORD · ALL-STAR GAME RECORD · ALL-STAR GAME RECORD · ALL-STAR GAME RECORD · ALL-STAR GAME RECORD

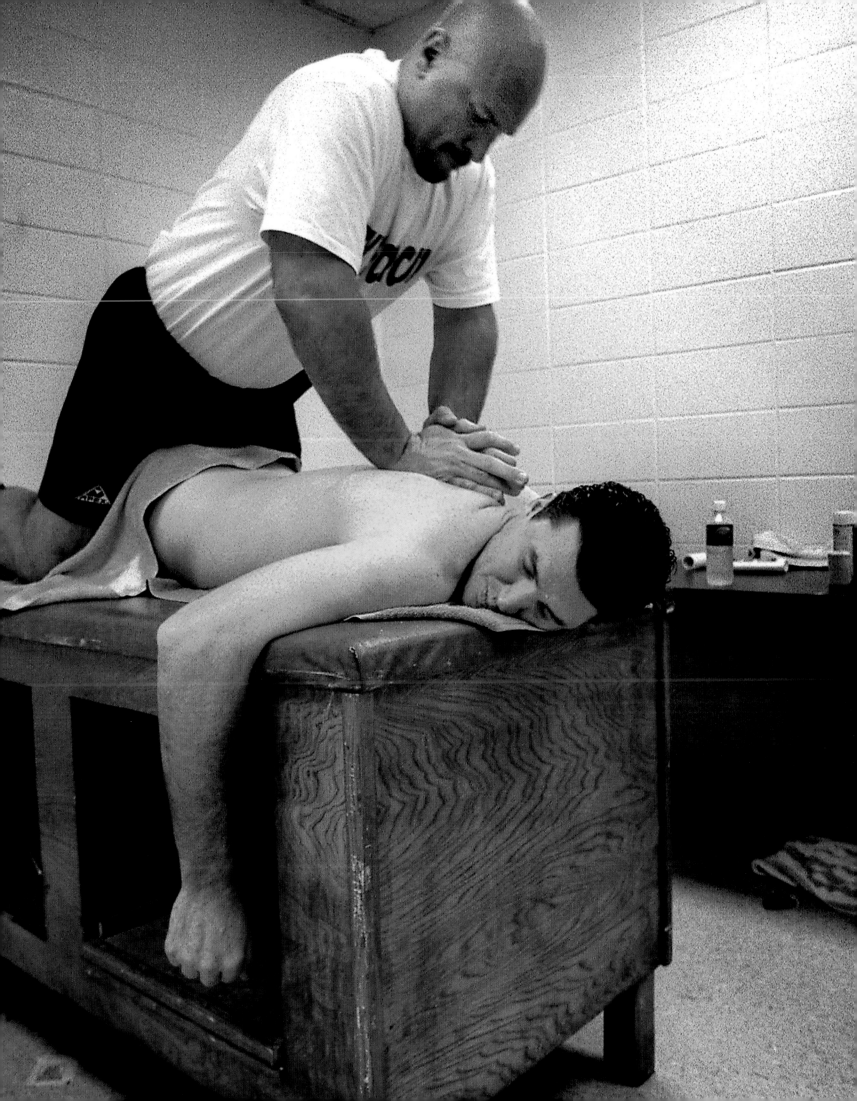

Actually, I started the 1989-90 season feeling great and playing well. It is ironic that during that time I put together the longest scoring streak of my NHL career—and the second-longest in league history—at 46 games. But for about the last 20 games of that streak, back pain was a major problem; I couldn't even tie my own skates, couldn't tie my own shoes. I probably was playing at less than 50 percent. I tried to fight through it, but, finally, during a game against the Rangers at New York on Feb. 14, I decided I just couldn't go any more. The streak ended at 46.

My agent, Tom Reich, arranged for me to fly to California to meet with the noted back specialist, Robert Watkins. Dr. Watkins put me on a program to try to improve my back condition without surgery, and I spent about six weeks in Los Angeles, working with members of his staff. But I certainly wasn't going to feel sorry for myself. It was only a back condition. Ashley Barrasso, the young daughter of our goaltender, Tom Barrasso, also was flown to Los Angeles to undergo treatments for cancer. That quickly put things in perspective for me and my teammates. Fortunately, young Ashley beat the dreaded disease.

With the help of Dr. Watkins—and after skating briefly with a few friends in L.A.—I actually was able to return for the final game of the regular season, when a tie would have put us in the playoffs. I managed to score a goal and an assist, but Buffalo pulled out a 3-2 victory in overtime to send us home for the summer. Finally, after experiencing some more pain—and after undergoing more medical consultations—it was determined that I would have back surgery in the off-season.

I underwent surgery to repair a herniated disk in Pittsburgh that July. The prognosis was optimistic; doctors thought I would be ready to join the team for training camp and be in the lineup for the start of the regular season. I was really looking forward to that season, which would be our first under new coach "Badger" Bob Johnson. It appeared that things finally were ready to turn around for the Penguins, thanks to an excellent management team of general manager Craig Patrick, director of player development Scotty Bowman, and Badger. Excitement was in the air.

back infection. I literally spent

the next three months on my

back, which was terrifying. We

didn't even know if I could play

again. It was a difficult time,

I came home the next day

and went right to the hospital.

I couldn't even stand up.

They did a test with a needle

to extract whatever is down

there, and that's when they

discovered that I had a rare

Fortunately, it all began to

clear up, the infection was

cured, and I was given the OK

to start skating in early January.

I resumed skating, resumed

practicing and accompanied

the team on a pre-season road

trip, which included a stop in

Houston. I remember that city

specifically because my back

had started to act up again, and

by the time we got to Houston

the pain was severe. It was

scary. I kept trying to stretch

and do my exercises, but the

more I did, the worse it got.

lying there on my back, knowing

I had an infection that was very

serious and could attack my

bones and spine. I tell you…

I did a lot of thinking.

MY FIRST GAME OF THE 1990-91 SEASON

CAME ON JAN. 26 IN QUEBEC.

WE WON, 6-5, AND I

PICKED UP THREE ASSISTS—

WHICH MAY HAVE
BEEN AN OMEN.

It took me a while to work myself into game shape, but I was delighted to be back on the ice again, and I definitely enjoyed playing for Badger. He was the best for picking up your confidence. Every day it was 'You guys are the best, you guys are great players.' He never said anything negative. Even when we lost games by five or six goals, he always found something positive to talk about. That was just Badger.

But our team was really struggling in late February, and we allowed 28 goals on a torturous five-game road trip, going 0-4-1. So as the trading deadline approached, Craig Patrick began working the phones. He pulled off a major six-player deal with the Hartford Whalers on the eve of the deadline, acquiring Ron Francis, Ulf Samuelsson and Grant Jennings in exchange for John Cullen, Zarley Zalapski and Jeff Parker. As it turned out, those were the final pieces to our championship puzzle.

We didn't exactly think it was going to be easy to win the Cup; remember, the Penguins had made the playoffs only one other time since 1982. But once we got Ronnie to stabilize our second line, and once we got Ulfie back there, we felt pretty confident. We thought we had a chance.

1991 STANLEY CUP CHAMPIONS

1992 STANLEY CUP CHAMPIONS

known in Pittsburgh sports lore five games. That set up a con- when we really started to believe up the series and clinching our

ference final showdown against first berth in the Stanley Cup

Boston, a veteran team steeped finals. I helped ice the victory

in tradition. The Bruins used with an empty-net goal late in

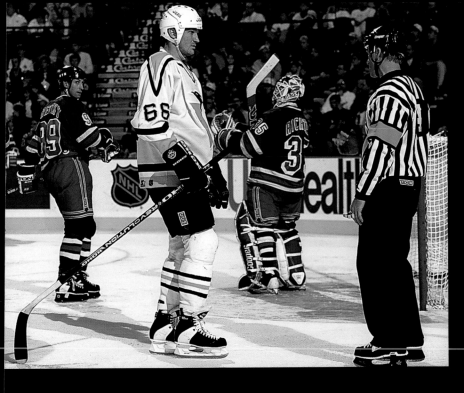

before the regular season that Craig named Scotty Bowman as interim coach.

Our team visited Badger at a Colorado Springs hospital during a pre-season road trip to Denver, and we left with heavy hearts. He couldn't speak because of his condition, but he was wearing a Penguins t-shirt and he was clearly excited to see "his" players. A lot of us wondered if it was the last time we would see him alive. In fact, it was.

Bob died in November, and the team held an emotional tribute to him before our next home game against New Jersey. There wasn't a dry eye on the ice, or in the house.

Craig Patrick called the players together and told us that Badger would want us to go on with our lives, play our best and win another Cup. I don't want to make it sound that simplistic, but Bob was in our thoughts the rest of the season.

We were struggling again until Craig pulled off another big trade, this time in February, acquiring Rick Tocchet, Kjell Samuelsson, Ken Wregget and Jeff Chychrun in a three-way deal with Philadelphia and Los Angeles. We finished only third in our division that year and trailed in each of our first two playoff series—by 3-1 to Washington and 2-1 to the New York Rangers. I suffered a broken hand when I was slashed by Adam Graves in Game 2 of the Rangers series. But our team pulled together and we rattled off 11 straight victories en route to our second straight Cup.

I was fortunate enough to return for Game 2 of the conference finals against Boston. We swept the Bruins to reach the finals against Chicago, then whipped the Blackhawks in four straight—although it wasn't as easy as it sounds. They built leads of 3-0 and 4-1 in Game 1 at Pittsburgh, and we didn't regain our equilibrium until Jaromir Jagr scored a terrific goal to tie it at 4-4, stepping off the left wing boards and beating three defenders, including all-star Chris Chelios.

I SAID AFTER THE GAME THAT IT WAS THE

GREATEST GOAL

I'D EVER SEEN.

We won it in the final seconds when I converted Larry Murphy's rebound and beat goalie Ed Belfour. We were on our way—again.

Our 1991-92 team could beat you any number of ways, using any number of styles, and we proved it in the series against the Hawks. We posted a 3-1 win in Game 2, a 1-0 victory in Game 3 and a 6-5 Cup-clincher in Game 4. Tighten it up. Run and gun. Didn't really matter.

We had another good skate with the Cup around Chicago Stadium, paying a little tribute to Badger along the way. But when people ask me to compare the championships, I have to tell them that the first one always is very special. To finally get there, after all those years, is amazing. The second time you kind of take it for granted, because you've already had the experience, and you have such a great team.

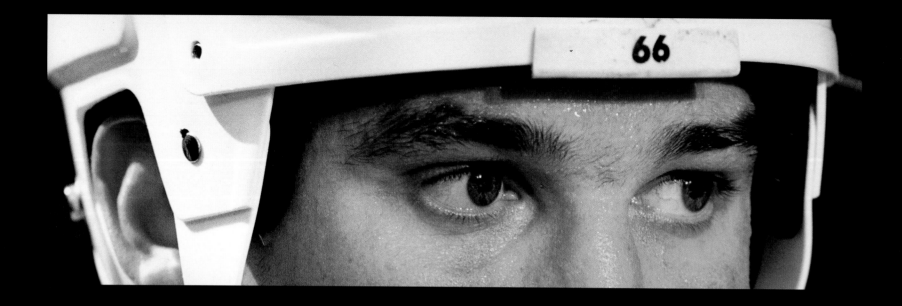

The 1992-93 season was going so well for me and for our team that I didn't anticipate any distractions.

We were running away with our division at mid-season, and I was playing on a great line with Kevin Stevens and Rick Tocchet and leading the scoring race. People were saying we should have ourselves fitted for more Stanley Cup rings. They were talking about a dynasty.

THEN CAME JANUARY 12, 1993, A DAY THAT CHANGED MY LIFE FOREVER.

To find out you have cancer—any type of cancer—is scary. When they told me I had Hodgkin's disease, it was probably the worst day of my life. I mean, everything was going so well, I was playing some good hockey, we had a chance to win another Cup, there were no worries…

THE NEWS WAS DEVASTATING FOR ME AND EVERYBODY INVOLVED.

Just the word cancer scares a lot of people. Speaking from personal experience, it is largely the fear of the unknown. I cried on the way home from the doctor's office, cried when I told Nathalie,

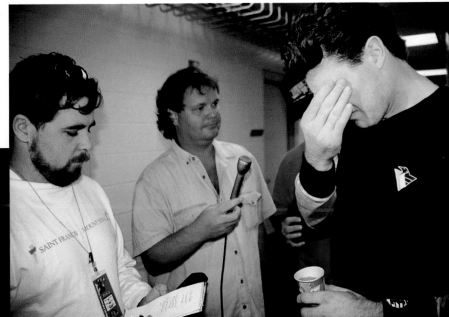

cried about my future. But the more I learned about what I was facing, the better I felt about the outcome. I talked to a few doctors as soon as it happened and I actually began to feel encouraged.

I wanted to keep skating with the team but I couldn't because of my radiation treatments. If I'd

gotten a cut on my neck, the radiation would be pushed back. I felt good until about the third week

of radiation, when I started to get tired and couldn't eat because I was too sore. When I came back

to the lineup after the treatments I felt a little bit tired, and then by the time the playoffs rolled around

I didn't have any gas.

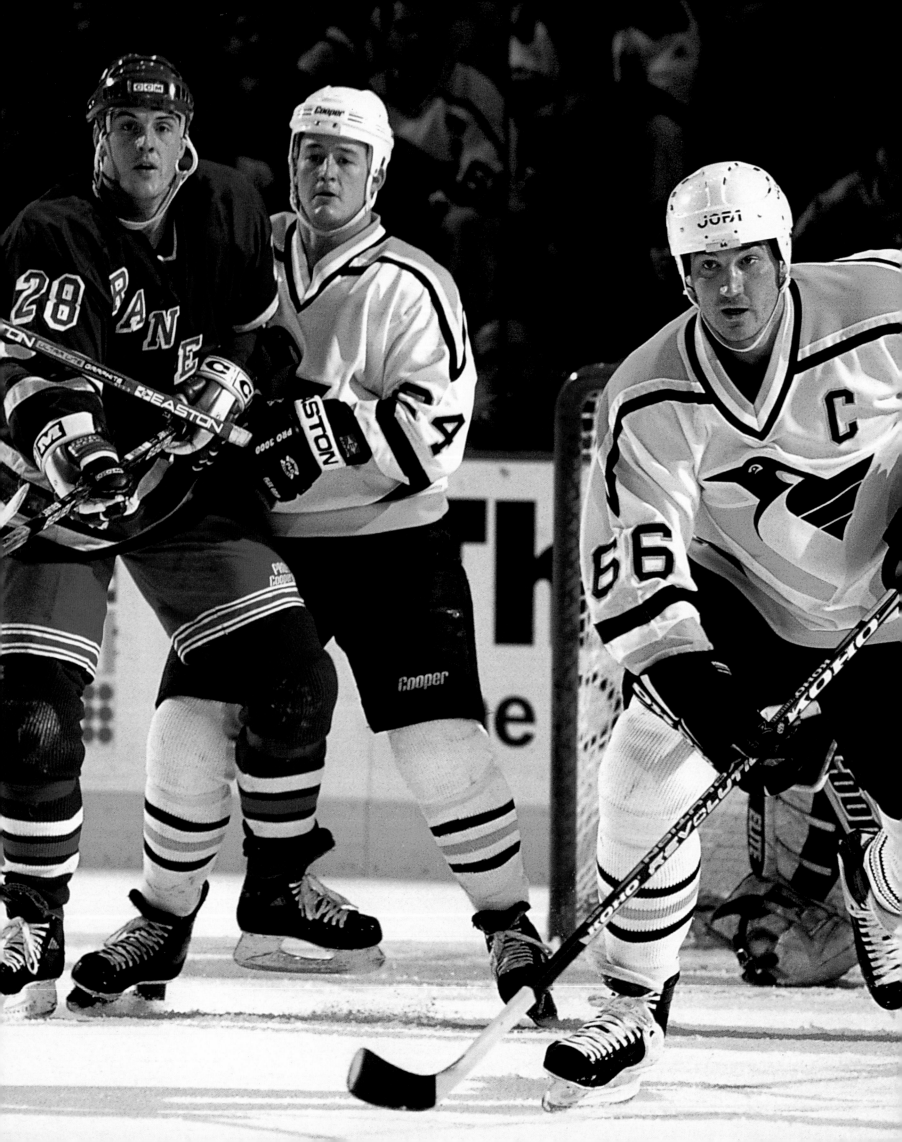

.823

HIGHEST GOALS PER
GAME AVERAGE
CAREER

I think I played really well for two or three weeks after coming back in March. I scored a goal in my first game back, at Philadelphia, where the normally hostile crowd gave me a warm standing ovation. I trailed Pat LaFontaine by something like 17 points in the scoring race, but I was able to catch him and pass him and win another scoring title. My best effort was getting five goals in a game against the Rangers at Madison Square Garden.

Our team set an NHL record with 17 straight victories late in the season, and we finished first in the overall standings with 56 wins and 119 points, both franchise records. One national publication referred to us as "unbeatable," but after we dispatched the New Jersey Devils in five games,

WE WERE **UPSET** IN THE SECOND ROUND BY THE FEISTY NEW YORK ISLANDERS.

David Volek scored in overtime in Game 7, as an odd silence settled over the Civic Arena. Our string of championships was snapped.

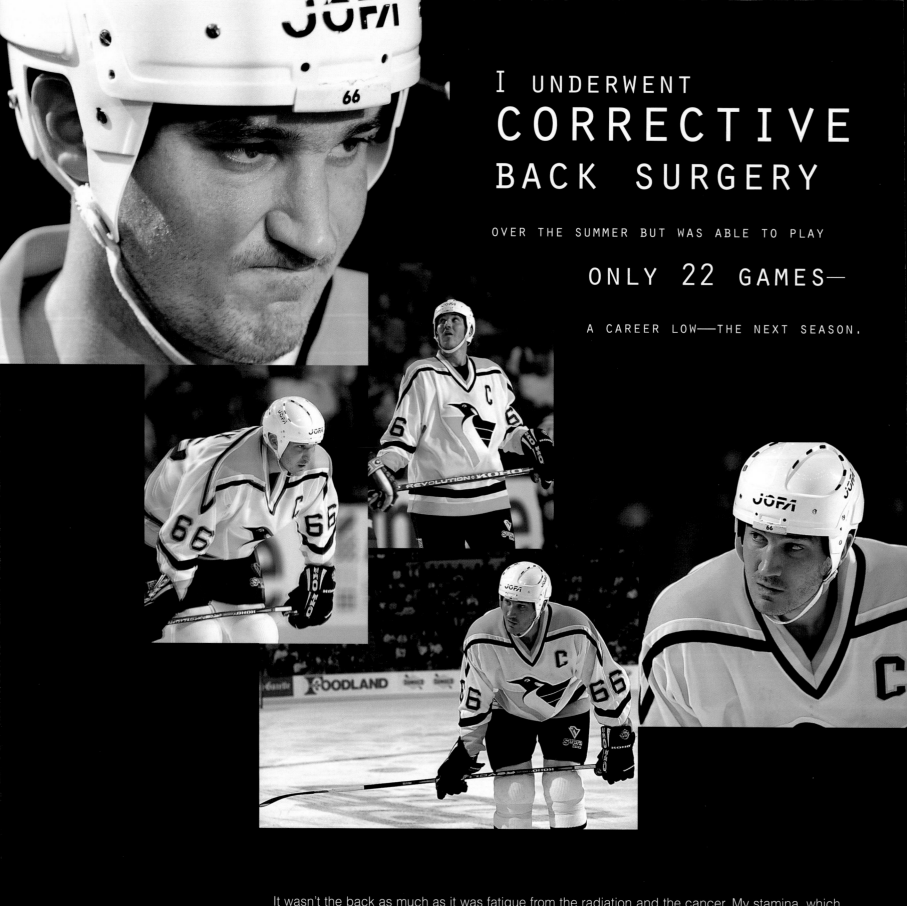

I UNDERWENT CORRECTIVE BACK SURGERY

OVER THE SUMMER BUT WAS ABLE TO PLAY

ONLY 22 GAMES—

A CAREER LOW—THE NEXT SEASON.

It wasn't the back as much as it was fatigue from the radiation and the cancer. My stamina, which

had always been there, wasn't the same. I wasn't able to perform. We were eliminated by Washington

in the first round of the playoffs and I made a decision to sit out the next season (1994-95) in an

attempt to rest and recuperate.

Believe me, I considered not coming back. And if I'd continued to feel the way I felt in November and December of 1994, there's no way I would have come back. But sitting out all year enabled me to recharge my batteries, and I really got the bug again while watching the '95 playoffs, when we beat Washington and then lost to the eventual champion, New Jersey. As I mentioned before, Nathalie also played a big role in my decision to come back. She wanted to see me back on the ice.

I started lifting weights for the first time in my life to prepare for the comeback. I worked three times a week with my trainer and massage therapist, Tom Plasko, lifting and doing a lot of bike work for leg strength. Before the cancer, my skating was always good, my legs were always strong, and my upper body was pretty strong even though I never lifted. But I was getting older, and my body had been through a lot. So I dedicated myself to the new workout program.

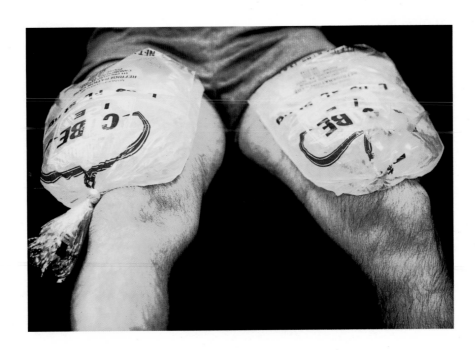

It was pretty amazing the way things worked out. We won our division again, established ourselves as a legitimate Cup contender, and I won my fifth career scoring title with 161 points. Despite all the health problems in my recent past, I was able to play 70 games—my highest total since 1988-89.

We beat Washington and the Rangers in the first two rounds of the playoffs but were eliminated by Florida in seven games in the conference finals. It was the closest we'd come to a Cup since winning our last one in 1992. As I headed into the off-season, however, I had some serious questions about my future in hockey. My body took much longer to recuperate and I had serious reservations if I'd be able to come back and play at a high level.

farewell

I was very close to not playing in 1996-97, closer than most people know. Until about two weeks before training camp, I didn't think I would be able to play. I thought my career was over.

I talked to Nathalie again, talked to my closest friends, and I decided to come back for one more year, to give it one more shot to win another Cup. But up until those last two weeks before camp, I probably was 99.9 percent sure that I wasn't going to play.

Then we went 6-13-1 in our first 20 games and it was very frustrating. We'd made so many changes in the summertime in an attempt to improve the team, and we felt the team was better, but nothing went right. I wasn't playing well. Nobody was playing well. The chemistry just wasn't there. Very frustrating.

But Craig made some big trades, a kid named Patrick Lalime came out of nowhere to strengthen our goaltending situation, we put together a couple of winning streaks—and for a while it looked like we had a chance. Still, we finished second in our division and were eliminated by Philadelphia in the first round of the playoffs. It just wasn't meant to be.

But I'm glad I came back. I was able to give it one more shot, and now I really know that it's time for me to step aside and go on with my life. It was important for me to come back and go through that experience and test myself that way. And I had some very special moments with my teammates and with the fans. I was able to score my 600th goal and 1,400th point during the season, and I even won my sixth career NHL scoring title.

The biggest question I had coming into the season was: Could I still do the things I was able to do before? And I think I answered that question. I was not able to play the way I once played. That is too frustrating for me. That is something I can't accept, because I have a very high standard for myself. Not being able to beat a guy one-on-one is something that is new to me. Throughout my career, even throughout my childhood, I always was able to beat a guy one-on-one. Once I couldn't do that any more I had to change my game. And I didn't enjoy the game as much.

I finally made my retirement announcement official during the Dapper Dan Dinner in Pittsburgh in early April. I didn't want to make the announcement early in the season, because I didn't want to become a distraction to everybody in every city along the way. I didn't want anything like a farewell tour. It's not my

personality. But by the time the Dapper Dan Dinner rolled around there were only a few games left in the regular season, and I wanted the team to be able to concentrate on the playoffs. I didn't want the question about my retirement to be an issue.

I got a tremendous ovation on my last trip to Montreal, my hometown. The Canadiens were nice enough to name me the No. 1 star, even though we lost the game. I got another stirring ovation from the fans in Boston, during the last game of the regular season. In a remarkable coincidence,

I PLAYED MY FIRST REGULAR SEASON GAME IN BOSTON AND MY LAST REGULAR SEASON GAME IN BOSTON.

The Bruins even gave me a seat from the old Boston Garden, the source of many memories as I head into retirement.

SAYING GOODBYE

And then there was my final game in Pittsburgh. April 23, 1997 at the Civic Arena. Game 4 of our first round series against the Flyers. Eerie.

We trailed in the series, three games to none, so everyone realized it might be my last game—or at least my last game on Pittsburgh ice. There were an astonishing number of signs with my name on them. It seemed that everyone was prepared—just in case.

The fans in Pittsburgh always have been tremendous to me and my family. They are a big part of the reason we plan to make our permanent home here. They were there for the Lemieux Debut on Oct. 17, 1984 and they were still there for me in April of 1997. At the very least, I was hoping to give them one last show.

Sure enough, we won the game, 4-1, pushing the series to a fifth game in Philadelphia. And the hockey gods smiled on me again. After receiving several thunderous ovations from the Arena crowd, I was fortunate enough to score a dramatic breakaway goal in the closing minutes. And the crowd was so loud, I swear the roof was shaking.

The Penguins public relations staff doctored the traditional three-star voting so that I was named the game's No. 1 star. And it gave me a chance to say goodbye to the fans. You never want to have to do something like that after you lose, but we had at least one more game in Philly. And I wanted to make sure I said goodbye to the fans, just in case we lost that game.

I didn't plan on taking that final lap around the rink. It was totally spontaneous. They told me to go out as the No. 1 star, but instead of taking my usual little swirl, I decided to go around the rink and thank the fans for a lot of great memories in 13 years. That was probably the first time I ever cried on the ice. And as I headed off for the dressing room, it really hit me that it might have been the last time

The whole scene was incredible. Even just having a *chance* to score a breakaway goal. People were chanting my name for the last five minutes of the game and I felt like they wanted me to do something special. I got the opportunity…and that was just icing on the cake.

ACKNOWLEDGING A STANDING OVATION IN PHILADELPHIA
DURING MY LAST GAME AGAINST THE FLYERS.

MY LAST GOAL CAME
ON A BREAKAWAY AGAINST
THE FLYERS IN THE
1997 PLAYOFFS.

70

PENGUINS RECORD · PENGUINS RECORD · PENGUINS RECORD · PENGUINS RECORD ·

MOST GOALS
IN PLAYOFF
CAREER

We went on to lose Game 5 in Philly, but the Flyers still named me the No. 1 star— a very classy move. I got a chance to speak privately to their great young star, Eric Lindros. I also stopped outside the dressing room to see my parents and family members who'd flown in for the game. And then it was over. One final bus to the airport. One final plane ride. From Ville Emard to Pittsburgh, from last place to the Stanley Cup, all the ups and downs along the way. It was over.

I was hoping to win one last Cup, but I think I accomplished every-

thing I wanted to in my career. Winning the two Cups, winning scoring

titles, the Canada Cup…I think I've achieved a lot of great things. As

I look back now, I feel very proud of what I've accomplished.

I JUST WANT TO SAY THANK YOU
TO ALL MY TEAMMATES AND COACHES,
WHO MADE IT POSSIBLE.
AND TO ALL MY FANS.
THANKS, AGAIN.

You've heard me talk about the state of the game many times. And so this is my last shot.

Hockey could be the greatest game in the world if only they let the great players be great.

It's really a shame that they're wasting a lot of great talent out there. The fans are being deprived by the state of the game. There is so much holding and hooking and grabbing and tackling that it is becoming increasingly difficult for the great offensive players to display their skills.

EXCITEMENT SELLS.
GOAL-SCORING SELLS.
OUR GAME WOULD BE A LOT MORE EXCITING
IF THEY OPENED THINGS UP,
THE WAY THEY DID IN BASKETBALL YEARS AGO.
RIGHT NOW, IT'S SIMPLY
NOT THE SAME GAME
I GREW UP WITH.

milestones

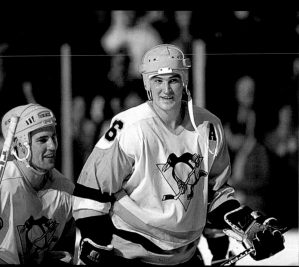

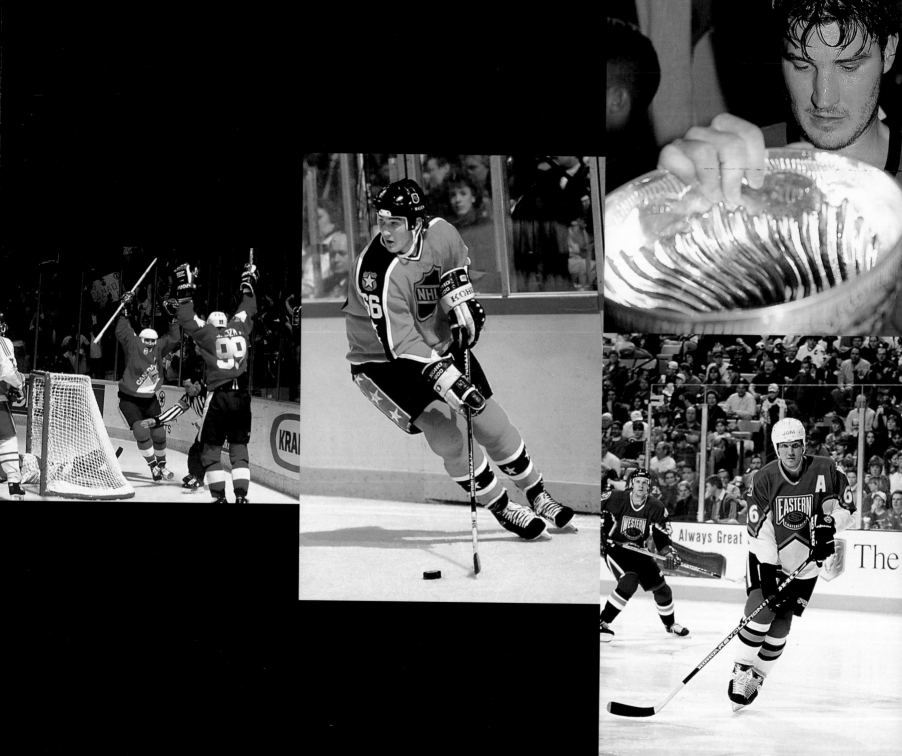

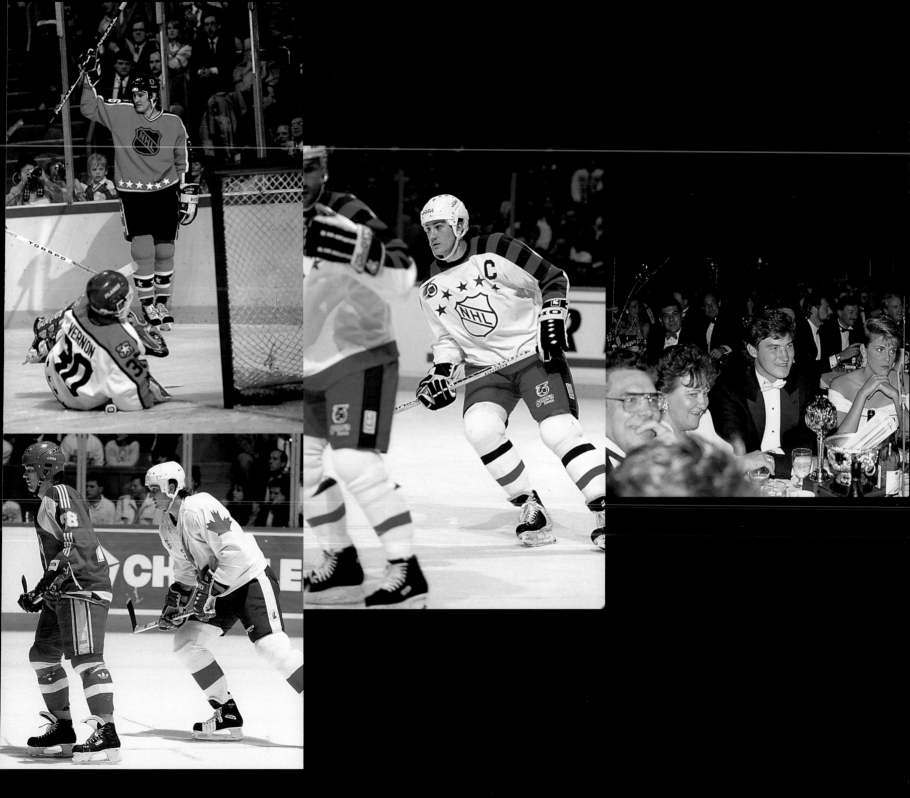

FEW MILESTONES WERE MORE MEMORABLE THAN
SCORING MY 600TH CAREER GOAL AT HOME.